AF584585

Migration to Australia

Migration From The Middle East and Africa

William Day

First published 2017 by
Redback Publishing
PO Box 357 Frenchs Forest NSW 2086
Australia

978-1-925630-10-7

Author: William Day
Editor: Margie Tubbs
Designer: Redback Publishing

MIX
Paper from responsible sources
FSC www.fsc.org
FSC® C020056

Original illustrations © Redback Publishing 2017
Originated by Redback Publishing

Printed and bound in China by Leo Paper

Acknowledgements
Abbreviations: l—left, r—right, b—bottom, t—top, c—centre, m—middle
We would like to thank the following for permission to reproduce photographs: (Images © shutterstock) p6 Boyloso , p11 MehmetO, p14 serkan senturk, p15 Owen_ Holdaway, p21 Anjo Kan, p22 thomas koch, p26 Sadik Gulec, p27 Sadik Gulec, p30 Vlad Karavaev

Every effort has been made to contact copyright holders of any material reproduced in this book. Any omissions will be rectified in subsequent printings if notice is given to the publisher.

National Library of Australia Cataloguing-in-Publication entry

Creator: Day, William, author.
Title: Migration from the Middle East and Africa / William Day.
ISBN: 9781925630107 (hardback)
Series: Migration to Australia.
Target Audience: For primary school age.
Subjects: Immigrants--Australia.
Australia--Emigration and immigration--Juvenile literature.
Middle East--Emigration and immigration--Juvenile literature.
Africa--Emigration and immigration--Juvenile literature.

Contents

Note on the Statistics
Not all countries hold a regular census.
Population figures and land territory sizes are estimates, based on official sources.

Reasons for Migration to Australia

Work
People have been arriving to work in Australia since pre-colonial times. Australia has needed migrants to provide the skills and labour for development since it was founded in 1788.

Family
Joining family members who have already migrated to Australia has been a strong pull factor in encouraging people to leave their country of birth.

Asylum
Wars and conflict around the world have caused thousands of people to seek asylum outside their own countries.

Religion
Freedom of religion is enshrined in the Australian Constitution. People who have suffered discrimination because of their religion have found that they can practise their religion freely in Australia.

Freedom
Australia is a stable democracy with freedom of speech, freedom to travel, equality for all and access to an independent legal system.

Home Ownership
Australia has a land ownership system that gives people assured title to property they have purchased. This is not the case in all countries.

Business
Australia provides educated workers and the infrastructure needed to set up successful businesses.

Education
Australian universities and colleges rank well compared with other countries. A degree from an Australian university is recognised in most countries around the world.

Health Care
Australian citizens and residents with appropriate visas have access to a health care system which provides free hospital care and treatment by a doctor who bulk-bills at no charge to the patient.

Lifestyle
Australia offers migrants a predominantly safe and friendly environment. Its beautiful landscapes and variety of climates, from tropical to alpine, attract both tourists and people wanting to settle permanently.

Top 10 Countries of Birth in Australia (2015)

Country of birth	Number of migrants	% of the Australian population
United Kingdom	1,207,000	5.1%
New Zealand	611,400	2.6%
China	481,800	2.0%
India	432,700	1.8%
Philippines	236,400	1.0%
Vietnam	230,200	1.0%
Italy	198,200	0.8%
South Africa	178,700	0.8%
Malaysia	156,500	0.7%
Germany	125,900	0.5%

In 2016, 28% of Australia's population were born overseas.

Challenges Faced by Migrants

Shopping

When a person cannot understand English well, grocery shopping can be stressful.

Health Care

Working out where to go for a health problem can be difficult when a person is not familiar with their surroundings.

Family

Not having any family nearby can make people feel lonely and isolated.

Lifestyle

Ways of living that are normal in one country may be criticised in others.

Education

Educational qualifications achieved in another country are not always recognised in Australia.

Emergencies

Seeking help in an emergency can be difficult if a person does not speak English well and does not know about the services available.

Legal System

Becoming familiar with Australia's legal system is a challenge to new migrants.

Transport

People need to work out how to use public and private transport without getting lost. This is complicated if a person has difficulty reading signs written in English.

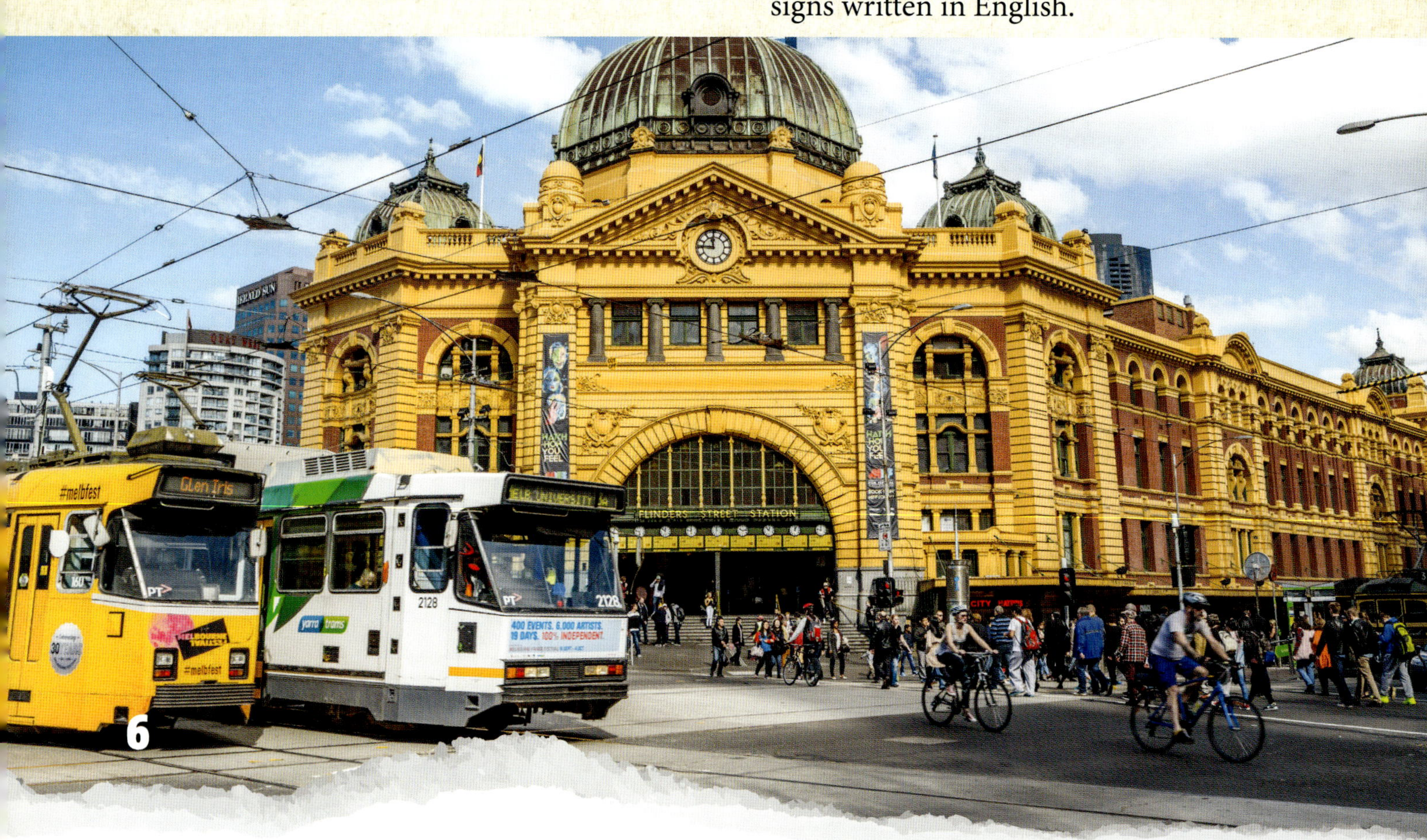

World Cultures

World cultures are divided by using terms that include:

Western, Eastern, Middle Eastern, Near Eastern, Asian, Polynesian

These adjectives refer to a lifestyle rather than a strictly-defined geographical region. At different times throughout history, some countries have been described by one or more of these terms.

Australia is called a 'western' country because of the way people live and the style of government, even though it is nowhere near western Europe.

World Geography

Countries of the world are grouped into geographic regions. The main ones are:

Europe, Middle East, Asia, Southeast Asia, Pacific, Oceania,
the Americas, North America, Africa

Political and religious events have resulted in some countries being classed in different regions throughout their history. For example, some people place Pakistan in the Middle East, while others locate it in Asia.

Workers and Skilled Migration

Australia has always needed to import workers. Initially, labour was provided by convicts but, after the late 1860s, they were no longer sent to Australia. The small population of Australia meant that there were not enough workers for farms, shops and industries.

Mass immigration programs were devised to encourage British and other European people to migrate to Australia. Despite these colonial migration schemes, there were still not enough workers. Up until 1901, when the White Australia Policy came into force, people from non-European countries were also allowed to come to Australia to work.

After World War II, another mass migration scheme from Europe provided the workers Australia lacked.

The selection of migrants to Australia today is based on hundreds of work categories for which there are not enough local skilled people to fill the available jobs. These categories change as the economy grows or contracts.

White Australia Policy

From 1901 to 1973, immigration to Australia was restricted by the White Australia Policy. The Australian government wanted to maintain Australia as an outpost of Great Britain, with a British culture and a population which was mostly British. Multiculturalism was not acceptable, and migrants from Europe were expected to assimilate, so that the British traditions that most Australians treasured would not be lost.

Migrants from Asia and other non-European places were thought to be too different in appearance and culture to ever be able to assimilate and make a contribution to the nation. In addition, Australian workers feared losing their jobs to people who might accept lower wages.

With increases in world travel, and the role of television and other mass media in increasing public awareness, Australia recognised that migrants from many countries would be able to settle harmoniously in Australia and contribute to its economy.

Commonwealth of Nations

The Commonwealth is a group of 52 nations. They meet every two years to discuss issues of common concern. Queen Elizabeth II is Head of the Commonwealth and head of state of 16 Commonwealth countries.

The Commonwealth was formed in 1949 as a group of countries with ties to Britain. This shared history is no longer a basis for membership. The latest two members, Rwanda and Mozambique, do not have a British colonial past.

Scholarships and fellowships are awarded by the United Kingdom to citizens of Commonwealth countries under the Commonwealth Scholarship and Fellowship Plan. The Commonwealth Games for athletes from member countries are held every four years.

Middle East

Afghanistan

Geography

Afghanistan is a country with deserts and semi-arid regions spread across mountains and plains. It is a source of oil, natural gas, minerals and gemstones. The borders of Afghanistan have changed throughout history. The capital city is Kabul.

Colonial History in Australia

In the 1800s, Afghan cameleers migrated to Australia. They provided a vital delivery service in remote, desert areas where their camels were better adapted to the climate than horses. Settlers living in these parts of Australia depended on the cameleers to supply them with household goods and provisions.

Unnamed Afghan men accompanied Australia's explorers and were often amongst the first non-Aboriginal people to see the country's desert landmarks.

The Overland Telegraph Line and the first railway running south to north were both constructed with the assistance of the Afghan cameleers. The rail service called The Ghan is now a tourist attraction, and was named after the Afghan cameleers.

With the development of motor vehicles, the cameleers eventually were no longer needed. Most of the Afghan men returned home, but some stayed in Australia, where they married and raised families. The remains of their small mosques still exist in a number of desert areas.

The oldest permanent mosque in Australia was funded by the Afghan cameleers. It was built in Adelaide in 1889.

20th Century in Australia

The first Afghan asylum seekers arrived in Australia after the invasion of Afghanistan by the USSR in 1979. After the Soviets left in 1989, another group of Afghan people arrived as escapees from the Taliban regime and the civil war. After 2000, more people left due to a severe drought. Most of the Afghan people who have come to Australia have settled in New South Wales and Victoria. The majority of Afghan people are Muslims.

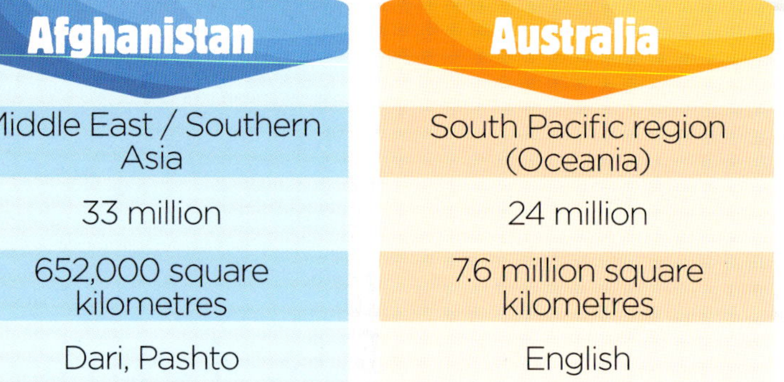

	Afghanistan	Australia
Location	Middle East / Southern Asia	South Pacific region (Oceania)
Population	33 million	24 million
Size	652,000 square kilometres	7.6 million square kilometres
Main Languages	Dari, Pashto	English

Afghan Culture

Nauroz

Nauroz is the Afghan New Year's Day. It is an ancient festival, and is also known as Farmers' Day. Nauroz is held in March to mark the beginning of the northern hemisphere spring.

Literature

Afghanistan has a long literary tradition of poetry, legends and storytelling, dating to well over a thousand years ago when royal courts fostered the arts.

Sport

Cricket - In 2013, Afghanistan qualified for their first Cricket World Cup. The country's team played in Australia in 2015.

Buzkashi - This Afghan sporting competition is held on horseback. It takes many years to master and both horse and rider need training to avoid injury. There can be up to 500 players on the field during a Buzkashi event. The aim of the game is to capture a calf and ride with it to the scoring area.

Australian-Afghan Business Council

The Australian-Afghan Business Council was formed in 2014 to promote business opportunities between the two countries.

UN Assistance Mission

The United Nations Assistance Mission in Afghanistan was established in 2002 at the request of the Government of Afghanistan.

Iran

Geography

Iran has large deserts in its centre. The densest population areas are in the north and along the coast of the Caspian Sea. Iran's most important resources are oil and gas. The capital city is Tehran.

Iranian History

Iran was once called Persia. About 2,500 years ago, Persia had a mighty empire and its archaeological remains are throughout Iran.

People

In the 1980s, the war between Iran and Iraq led to people leaving Iran, seeking to settle in other countries.

From the 1990s, professional people from Iran migrated to Australia to seek a different lifestyle. Many found that they needed to take extra education courses before their qualifications were accepted.

Higher education for women is often encouraged amongst families in Iran who can afford it, although there are some gender-based restrictions. The 2011 Australian census showed that people with Iranian heritage had a higher rate of tertiary education than for the rest of the Australian population.

New South Wales has the biggest Iranian community in Australia.

Religion

People of the Baha'i religion arrived in Australia under a humanitarian program from 1981. Other Iranian migrants include Muslims and Christians.

Culture

Food Iranian cuisine is not hot or overly spicy. It includes ingredients such as saffron, rose-water and preserved lemons, creating a mix of delightful flavours.

Nowruz This spring festival is held in March. It marks the Persian New Year.

Clothing In Iran, there are dress codes for men and women: men should not wear shorts or sleeveless tops and women must wear a headscarf and long, loose clothing.

	Iran	Australia
Location	Middle East	South Pacific region (Oceania)
Population	83 million	24 million
Size	1.5 million square kilometres	7.6 million square kilometres
Main Languages	Persian (Farsi)	English

Baha'i Temple on Sydney's Northern Beaches

Iraq

Geography
Iraq has flat plains and large desert regions. There are mountains in the north where snow falls in the winter. The Tigris and Euphrates Rivers flow through Iraq. Between these two rivers is the site where archaeologists believe humans first began to engage in agriculture. Oil provides 95% of the country's income. The capital city is Baghdad.

Religion
The majority of people in Iraq are Arabs and Kurds and they are mostly Muslim. In Australia's 2011 census, the majority of people who had come from Iraq were Christians, with Muslims being the next largest group. Assyrian Christians in Australia have formed a strong community which is proud of its ancient history in Iraq. The Assyrian New Year, which begins in April, is celebrated widely in Australia.

People
War and ethnic disputes have resulted in thousands of Iraqi people becoming displaced and seeking asylum in other countries. In the past decade, the largest number of visas under Australia's offshore humanitarian program was granted to people from Iraq. Recent arrivals have also been allowed entry under skilled migration and family reunion schemes. Most of the Iraqi settlers now live in New South Wales and Victoria.

Australians in Iraq
Australia provides a high level of overseas aid to people in Iraq, with the aim of improving their standard of living and security. Iraq remains a dangerous country and the Australian government advises against any travel there. Travel to some parts of Iraq is an offence under Australian law.

	Iraq	Australia
Location	Middle East	South Pacific region (Oceania)
Population	38 million	24 million
Size	437,000 square kilometres	7.6 million square kilometres
Main Languages	Arabic	English

Australia's Security

From the Australian Department of Foreign Affairs and Trade:

> *"Australians risk prosecution under Australian law if they engage in a hostile activity in a foreign country, or enter a foreign country with the intention of engaging in a hostile activity."*

At 2017, this law applied to some regions of Iraq and Syria.

Israel

About Israel

Israel was formed in 1948 under a United Nations resolution to give Jewish people a homeland. The Israeli Embassy in Canberra was established in the same year. There have been a number of wars and ongoing disputes over territory in Israel since its founding.

Israel has an advanced and growing economy, and there are close diplomatic and trade ties with Australia. Under an agreement between the governments of Australia and Israel, a limited number of young people are allowed to travel on working holidays between the two countries each year. Three quarters of Israel's population are Jewish.

Israelis in Australia

Jewish people, including Holocaust survivors, sought to start a new life in many countries, including both Australia and Israel, after World War II.

People from Israel have chosen to move to Australia to avoid the threat of armed conflict and to join family members. According to the 2011 census, there were about 9,000 people in Australia who were born in Israel. The majority of them lived in Victoria and New South Wales.

There is also a stream of Jewish emigrants from Australia to Israel, where they can practise their religion surrounded by people of the same faith. Many Jewish Australians visit Israel regularly and have family members who live there.

	Israel	Australia
Location	Middle East	South Pacific region (Oceania)
Population	8 million	24 million
Size	20,000 square kilometres	7.6 million square kilometres
Main Languages	Hebrew	English

Palestinian Territories

The Palestinian Territories include the West Bank and the Gaza Strip, a combined area of about 6,000 square kilometres. Australia provides overseas development aid to Palestinian people in these areas and also works with the United Nations to assist Palestinian people in refugee camps. Part of Australia's aid has enabled girls and boys to receive an education and improve water and sanitation in schools.

UNRWA

The United Nations Relief and Works Agency is the official body which provides assistance to five million Palestinian refugees. It has been operating since 1950 and now has 30,000 staff. As well as providing aid within the two Palestinian Territories, UNRWA also administers refugee services in Jordan, Lebanon and Syria.

Lebanon

Geography

Lebanon borders the Mediterranean Sea. The Lebanon Mountains run through the centre of the country. The capital city is Beirut.

Migration

A few people from Lebanon arrived in colonial Australia, where many worked in the clothing industry and set up businesses in rural New South Wales. Colonial records usually refer to them as Turks or Syrians. Larger numbers, who were mostly Christians, arrived after World War II.

The civil war from 1975 to 1990 resulted in the death or displacement of thousands of Lebanese people and led to a large group of Lebanese migrants seeking settlement in Australia.The Australian government eased immigration restrictions at this time to allow those already in Australia to bring family members from Lebanon to join them. Most of the people with Lebanese heritage in Australia live in New South Wales and are predominantly Muslims or Christians.

The Cedar Tree

Cedar forests grow in the Lebanon Mountains and the cedar tree is the country's national emblem. Cedar wood from Lebanon was used by ancient civilisations and is frequently mentioned in biblical texts. Today, Lebanese businesses, social and sporting groups use references to the cedar tree to show pride in their homeland.

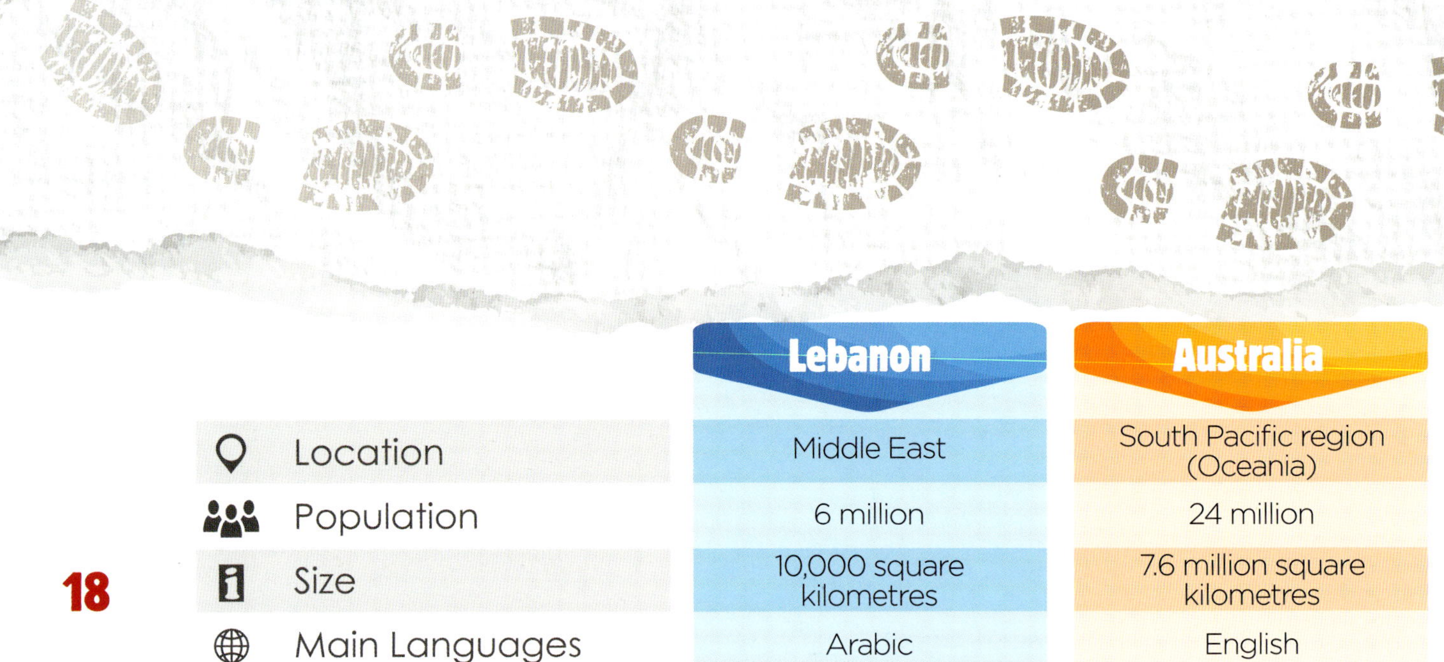

	Lebanon	Australia
Location	Middle East	South Pacific region (Oceania)
Population	6 million	24 million
Size	10,000 square kilometres	7.6 million square kilometres
Main Languages	Arabic	English

Cedar forest in Lebanon

Pakistan

Geography

Arid, hot regions exist across large parts of Pakistan. In the north, the country reaches the Himalayan mountains. Pakistan has a history dating back 5,000 years to the beginnings of the prehistoric Indus Valley civilisation. Islamabad is the capital city.

People

The majority of people in Pakistan are Muslims. The Pakistani community in Australia is also mostly Muslim. Pakistani students attend Australian tertiary education institutions and have received scholarships under the Australia Awards. The New Colombo Plan has given Australian students the chance to study in Pakistan.

Recent migrants to Australia from Pakistan have arrived under skilled migration schemes and there is a large proportion of professional people among them. New South Wales and Victoria have been their main destinations. There were 41,500 Pakistan-born people living in Australia in 2013.

	Pakistan	Australia
Location	Middle East, Southern Asia	South Pacific region (Oceania)
Population	202 million	24 million
Size	771,000 square kilometres	7.6 million square kilometres
Main Languages	Urdu, Punjabi	English

Shared Love of Cricket

One of the outcomes of Australia's shared Commonwealth history with Pakistan is that both nations are avid cricket fans.

National Holiday

Yaum-e-Pakistan (Pakistan Day)is a national holiday held on 23 March to commemorate Pakistan becoming the world's first Islamic republic in 1956.

Syria

Geography

There are large semi-arid and desert areas throughout Syria. Its capital city is Damascus, one of the oldest continuously occupied cities in the world. Syria has a diverse population with people of many ethnicities and religions.

People

Syrian people have been living in Australia since the 1800s. Syria was once part of the Ottoman Empire, so colonial records in Australia recorded people coming from Syria as Turks. Since the 1960s, and before the refugee crisis, migrants from Syria mainly arrived in Australia through family reunion schemes.

In 2011, a civil war broke out in Syria. This war has resulted in the world's largest humanitarian crisis since World War II. Millions of Syrian people have been left homeless and many have sought safety in United Nations refugee camps in nearby countries. Some Syrians have tried to come to Australia by boat or have journeyed to countries in Western Europe, hoping they will be allowed to stay.

In 2015, the Australian Government increased the number of permanent visas it offers to people fleeing as a result of the conflict in Syria and Iraq and who are in Turkey, Lebanon or Jordan.

Australia also provides assistance within Syria to help the people there. Funding to assist education aims to improve the future prospects of Syrians, both in their own country and in other nearby places where they are living as refugees.

	Syria	Australia
 Location	Middle East	South Pacific region (Oceania)
 Population	17 million	24 million
 Size	184,000 square kilometres	7.6 million square kilometres
Main Languages	Arabic	English

Turkey

Geography

The capital of Turkey is Istanbul, which used to be called Constantinople. Situated on the route of the ancient Silk Road, Turkey has been a meeting place for western and eastern cultures for thousands of years.

People

Turkish people already in Australia were interned during World War I, along with Germans and Austrians. In 1967, Australia had a special migration agreement with Turkey. As a result, Turkish migrants became the first large group of Muslim people to settle in Australia. Victoria and New South Wales were their main destinations.

Gallipoli

Turkey has a close relationship with Australia. Gallipoli is a special place for Australians and the focus of ANZAC Day commemorations. Although the two countries were opponents during World War I, the Turkish government and people now join the ANZAC Day ceremonies at Gallipoli, and assist Australians who travel there each April.

	Turkey	Australia
Location	Middle East, Europe	South Pacific region (Oceania)
Population	80 million	24 million
Size	770,000 square kilometres	7.6 million square kilometres
Main Languages	Turkish	English

Republic Day

Turkish Republic Day is celebrated on 28 October to mark the founding of the Republic of Turkey in 1923. Mustafa Kemal Ataturk was its first President.

Auburn Gallipoli Mosque

The Auburn Gallipoli Mosque was financed mostly by Turkish migrants. It is named in honour of the close relationship that has developed between Turkey and Australia as a result of events at Gallipoli in World War I.

The mosque was completed in 1999 and is listed by the National Trust, an organisation which works to conserve places of national heritage.

Auburn Gallipoli Mosque in Auburn, Sydney, Australia

Africa

Egypt

Geography

The capital city of Egypt is Cairo, located on the banks of the Nile River. Beyond the river banks, Egypt has large desert regions.

People

Most of the people with Egyptian heritage in Australia live in New South Wales and Victoria. They are mainly Christians, in contrast to Egypt where Islam is the largest religion. It was rare for Egyptians to emigrate permanently until the 1970s, when the Egyptian government made it easier for its citizens to seek work overseas.

Australians have been taking holidays to Egypt for decades, to see the pyramids and the Sphinx. However, recent unrest in Egypt has caused the Australian government to advise against travel.

		Egypt	Australia
	Location	Northern Africa	South Pacific region (Oceania)
	Population	95 million	24 million
	Size	995,000 square kilometres	7.6 million square kilometres
	Main Languages	Arabic	English

Somalia

Geography

Somalia is in sub-Saharan Africa and occupies the area known as the Horn of Africa. Its capital city is Mogadishu.

History

Somalia was formed in 1960 after the withdrawal of colonial powers in the area. There has been continuous civil unrest in the country since then, as well as periods of famine. Somalia is one of the top three sources of the world's asylum seekers, along with Afghanistan and Syria. Australia's humanitarian aid to Somalia is delivered through the United Nations.

People

A small number of Somali students arrived in Australia in the 1980s. Refugees were accepted in the 1990s and, more recently, Somali people have joined family members in Australia under the family migration scheme. The largest Somali community lives in Melbourne. The majority of Somali people are Muslims.

	Somalia	Australia
Location	Eastern Africa	South Pacific region (Oceania)
Population	11 million	24 million
Size	627,000 square kilometres	7.6 million square kilometres
Main Languages	Somali	English

Australian Aid

Australia's aid program to sub-Saharan Africa concentrates on four points of action:

- leadership
- agriculture
- humanitarian crises
- gender equality to empower women and girls

South Africa

Geography

Johannesburg is the largest city in South Africa. There is no single capital city and Pretoria, Cape Town and Bloemfontein share the role.

People

Immigrants of European background have been arriving in Australia from the area now known as South Africa since colonial times. They increased in number after the 1960s, following civil unrest in South Africa. After the 1970s, South African people of different ethnicities were also welcomed into Australia.

The South African population in Australia is generally highly educated and involved in business and the professions.

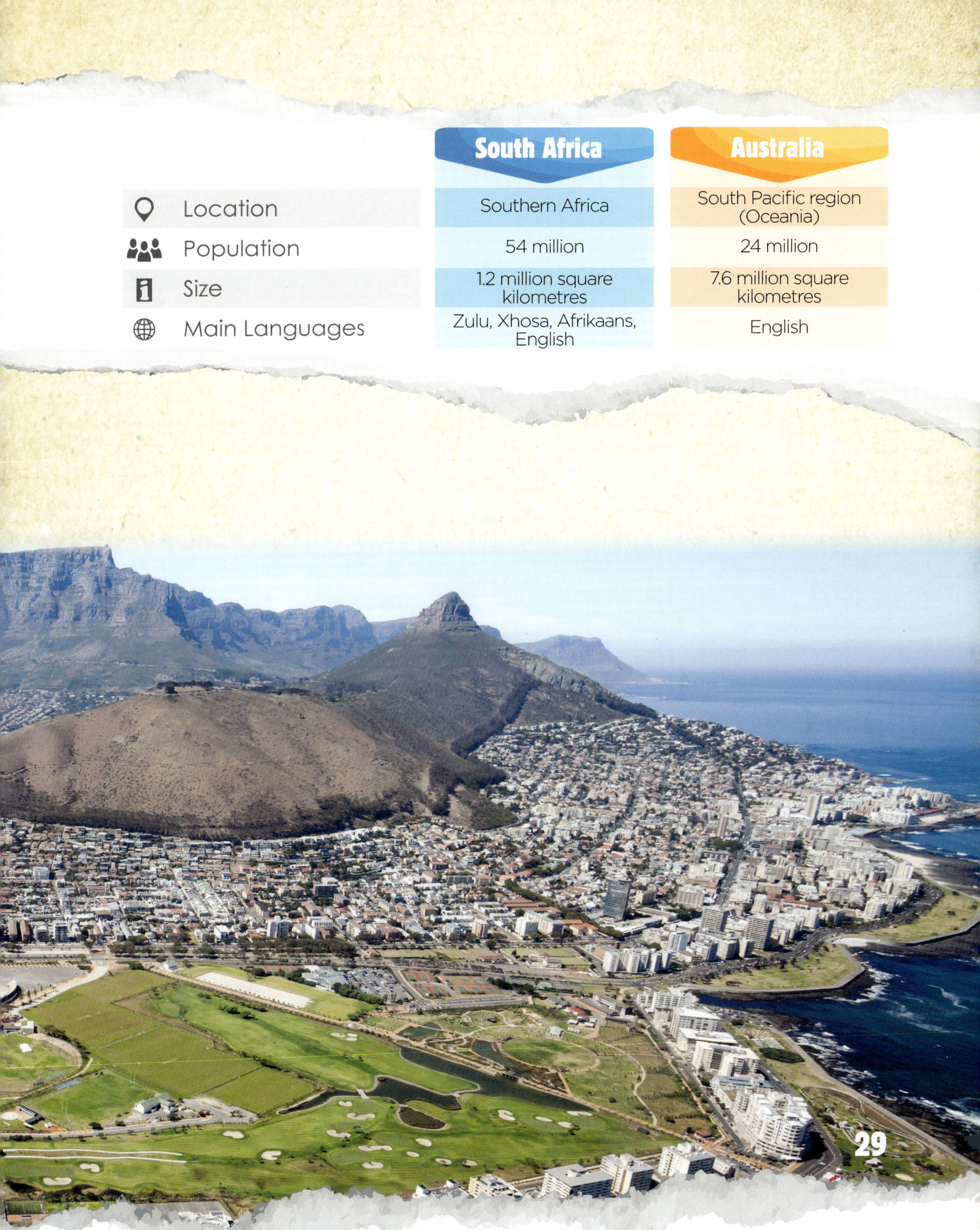

	South Africa	Australia
Location	Southern Africa	South Pacific region (Oceania)
Population	54 million	24 million
Size	1.2 million square kilometres	7.6 million square kilometres
Main Languages	Zulu, Xhosa, Afrikaans, English	English

South Sudan and Sudan

South Sudan

In 2011, South Sudan became an independent country. Internal conflict continued and has resulted in the displacement of many people. South Sudan has a diverse population whose religions include traditional faiths and Christianity. Its capital city is Juba.

In Australia, the majority of people with South Sudanese heritage are Christians and the main language spoken is Dinka.

Australia has contributed defence force personnel to assist the United Nations Mission in the Republic of South Sudan (UNMISS).

Sudan

Sudan is in northern Africa and its capital city is Khartoum. The majority of people in Sudan are Muslim and speak Arabic.

The Nile River runs through the centre of the country, which depends on its waters for agriculture. There are arid regions beyond the Nile River plains.

Political disputes, civil war and drought have affected Sudan for many years, resulting in Sudanese people leaving their country and becoming asylum seekers in refugee camps in other countries.

New South Wales Contingent

In 1885, the New South Wales Contingent left to fight with the British against an uprising in Sudan. This was the first overseas military force raised by an Australian colony.

Visit these websites to find out more about migration to Australia from the Middle East and Africa:

www.migrationheritage.nsw.gov.au
www.emelbourne.net.au
www.sbs.com.au/immigrationnation

Glossary

archaeology	the study of the remains of human societies
assimilate	to become part of a group
displacement	not being able to live in your home, due to war or civil unrest
famine	widespread lack of food, leading to starvation
infrastructure	organisations, buildings and equipment needed for a large project
interned	sent to camps as enemies during wartime
property title	confirmation of ownership of a property

Index